This book is published by The Aetherius Society, a Religious, Educational and Charitable Organization.

THE AUTHOR

Doctor George King who, acting in the capacity of "Primary Terrestrial Mental Channel," served as the annalist for this book. He received his first contact with Interplanetary Intelligences in 1954 and has since taken more than 600 Transmissions from The Cosmic Masters.

OPERATION SPACE MAGIC
THE COSMIC CONNECTION

BY
GEORGE KING, Ph.D., D.Litt.

Published by
THE AETHERIUS SOCIETY
6202 Afton Place, Hollywood, California 90028-8298. U.S.A.

First Published — 1982.

Copyright owned by George King, Ph.D., D.Litt.

Copyright ©1982 by George King, Ph.d., D.Litt.

All rights reserved. No reproduction or translation in whole or part of *"Operation Space Magic — The Cosmic Connection"* is allowed without written permission from the author, George King, Ph.D., D.Litt.

OPERATION SPACE MAGIC — THE COSMIC CONNECTION is published by The Aetherius Society, 6202 Afton Place, Hollywood, California 90028-8298. U.S.A.

Manufactured in the United States of America

OPERATION SPACE MAGIC
THE COSMIC CONNECTION

Written by

GEORGE KING, Ph.D., D.Litt.

By the same author:

    THE NINE FREEDOMS
    THE DAY THE GODS CAME
    THE TWELVE BLESSINGS
    VISIT TO THE LOGOS OF EARTH
    YOU TOO CAN HEAL
    YOU ARE RESPONSIBLE!
    THE THREE SAVIOURS ARE HERE
    THE FIVE TEMPLES OF GOD
    THE AGE OF AETHERIUS
    OPERATION SUNBEAM — GOD'S MAGIC IN ACTION
    WISDOM OF THE PLANETS
    LIFE ON THE PLANETS
    COSMIC VOICE, VOLUME NO. 1
    COSMIC VOICE, VOLUME NO. 2
    BECOME A BUILDER OF THE NEW AGE
    THIS IS THE HOUR OF TRUTH
    JOIN YOUR SHIP
    A COSMIC MESSAGE OF DIVINE OPPORTUNITY
    MY CONTACT WITH THE GREAT WHITE BROTHERHOOD
    SPACE CONTACT IN SANTA BARBARA
    THE ATOMIC MISSION
    A SPECIAL ASSIGNMENT
    CONTACT YOUR HIGHER SELF THROUGH YOGA
    THE PRACTICES OF AETHERIUS
    THE FLYING SAUCERS
    A SERIES OF LESSONS ON SPIRITUAL SCIENCE ON CASSETTES

(A price catalogue with complete list of books and cassettes by the same author is available upon request)

All books and cassettes by George King, Ph.D. are obtainable from the publishers, The Aetherius Society, American Headquarters, 6202 Afton Place, Hollywood, California 90028-8298. U.S.A., or from the European Headquarters of The Aetherius Society at 757 Fulham Road, London SW6 5UU, England.

DEDICATION

This book is respectfully dedicated to The Six Adepts, to Whom terrestrials owe so much.

CONTENTS

	Pages
INTRODUCTION TO THE AUTHOR	11-16
FOREWORD	17-19
AUTHOR'S RECOMMENDATIONS	20-21
VEHICLE DATA	25-30
AUTHOR'S RECOMMENDATIONS	31-32
OPERATIONAL PHASE LOG — PHASE ONE	33-42
AUTHOR'S RECOMMENDATIONS	43-44
OPERATIONAL PHASE LOG — PHASE TWO	45-54
OPERATIONAL PHASE LOG — PHASE THREE	55-64
OPERATIONAL PHASE LOG — PHASE FOUR	65-74
OPERATIONAL PHASE LOG — PHASE FIVE	75-85
CONCLUSION	86-91
AUTHOR'S RECOMMENDATIONS	92-93

INTRODUCTION TO THE AUTHOR

The author of this book was born in Shropshire, England, on January 23rd, 1919. Even from an early age he became interested in Religion, at first of an orthodox nature. Later, when he carefully studied what is known today as the metaphysical sciences, he turned to the close study and diligent practice of certain forms of Yoga. This mystical science was the evolutionary ladder up which he climbed in order to learn about the higher aspects of the multitudinous forms of life which abound on this Planet. Thus, without his realization at that time, he was preparing himself for a major step forward which was due to change the whole of his life and allow him to throw his intensity of purpose and dedication in a direction which would prove to be of great benefit to mankind.

In 1954, out of the blue, came the first Contact, recognizable as such, with Cosmic Intelligences Who lived in other parts of the Solar System. The story of this Contact has been written up by the media, hundreds of times in many different languages. It has been repeated hundreds of times by lecturers on the public platforms throughout the United States, England, Nigeria, New Zealand, Australia, Holland and other European countries.

From that initial Contact the author, already capable of bringing about the deep meditative state of Samadhi, was used as a mental channel for over 600 Transmissions given by Intelligences residing on more highly evolved worlds than this Earth. Some of these Transmissions have been published both in the written word and on cassettes which have circulated throughout many countries and have brought enlightenment and hope to thousands of people.

In 1955 The Aetherius Society was founded by the author in England, and later incorporated in the United States in 1960. Since that time The Aetherius Society has been responsible for the preservation and publication of these great Cosmic Transmissions, all of which are Teachings of profundity and yet given in a way which can be understood by any thinking researcher.

As well as being made responsible for receiving Cosmic Transmissions, the author was also given many other assignments by Cosmic Intelligences. These are fully described in literature published by The Aetherius Society.

Early in 1966 he invented and designed a Mission which was to become world renowned for its importance. This Mission was officially named "Operation Sunbeam" and accepted into the overall Cosmic Plan for the advancement, enlightenment and salvation of mankind. Although described in detail elsewhere, briefly, "Operation Sunbeam" is a Mission in which Spiritual Energies of the highest frequency are collected and these are given, through certain known Psychic Centres of Earth, to The Logos Of Earth as a token energy repayment for what this mighty Cosmic Being has done for all life on this Planet.

Man is completely dependent upon the Planet Earth for his present existence. Although he has taken all the sustenance and riches he possibly can from the Body of this Planet, seldom throughout the centuries has he made any concerted attempt to even thank God, the Creator, and the Logos for Her great sacrifice on his behalf. The author designed "Operation Sunbeam" as a modus operandi through which Spiritual Energies could be given back to the Logos as a representation of what man should have done throughout the centuries.

Although "Operation Sunbeam" did not receive the fame it deserves on this Planet, however, observers from other worlds soon learnt about it and started their own equivalents of this great Mission to their respective Logoi. It should be understood that advanced People on other Planets were already performing a similar sacrifice; however, those who were not took heart from the fact that, if a sacrifice of Spiritual Energy to a Logos could be performed correctly by a small, skilled group of individuals on a Planet inhabited by life forms as backward as those on Earth, then they could and should perform it in their own way on their own worlds. According to Cosmic Sources — not our idea — "Operation Sunbeam" started one of the biggest Spiritual snowballs in the history of this Galaxy!

The author has made the statement very often that it was because he gave his life in unconditional surrender to God that he was so inspired by the God-Force within that he was able to formulate a Mission such as "Operation Sunbeam."

For years, a small, carefully chosen, dedicated team of Staff Members of The Aetherius Society, under the guidance and strict discipline imposed by the designer of "Operation Sunbeam," worked to make this Operation a success. Other eyes in this Solar System, and even beyond, were upon the author all this time.

Seven years ago, in 1975, The Six Adepts started to build Modules and a Satellite which could, in future, help "Operation Sunbeam" and other Operations, to become even more potent than these had been in the past. This book gives a brief account of the action of The Six Adepts to bring this about.

As well as designing "Operation Sunbeam" and all the equipment necessary for its correct function, the author guided The Aetherius Society so that, for its size, it could become one of the most active Religious, educational and humanitarian societies of its kind on Earth. He worked tirelessly for years, sometimes to the detriment of his own health and strength, to help mankind, without the outside recognition he richly deserved.

Even so, there was a vast and controlled Plan being put into operation by both the Cosmic Masters from other worlds and the Spiritual Hierarchy of Ascended Masters on this Earth. The author had been instructed to hold himself in readiness for an invitation to an assembly arranged by the Highest Powers on this Earth in order to extend the range, potency and possibilities of the Mission, "Operation Sunbeam", which he had designed.

At approximately 2:00 p.m. on December 5th, 1978, the call came.

The author, well-versed in certain advanced Yogic techniques, was able to project his consciousness from his physical body and was received with love and understanding by the Members of the Spiritual Hierarchy of Earth in that mystical floating Temple called "Shamballa", which, for thousands of years, has been the Headquarters through which the Spiritual Hierarchy of this Earth operate. Like the Elevated Beings They are, They also respect true protocol in all its forms.

The main reason for the invitation was to ask permission of the designer of "Operation Sunbeam" if They, the Spiritual Hierarchy of Earth, may advance "Operation Sunbeam" in such a way which would not be possible for The Aetherius Society with its limited funding and resources. The author, strictly obeying what may be termed as "mystical protocol", enquired first if these Masters had gained permission from even Higher Authority before the question was posed. Having been assured that the correct protocol had been observed in every minute detail, the author was then put in the singular position of giving his permission to the Ascended Masters for the extension of "Operation Sunbeam" as They proposed and further, permission to adopt the basic modus operandi which the author had discovered through painstaking research.

After this, much to the utter amazement of the author, he was then approached by the Kumara of Shamballa, Who physically touched him three times: once upon the head, then upon the right shoulder and then upon the left shoulder, and spoke in a physical voice in perfect English, these most significant words:

"I thus initiate you as Grand Knight Templar of the Inner Sanctum of the Holy Order of the Spiritual Hierarchy of Earth."

This mystical Knighthood was bestowed upon the author for his devotion and co-operation with the Cosmic Masters since 1954 and especially for his work in "Operation Sunbeam", which helped to bring about a stabilization of conditions on the Planet Earth. (Read The Aetherius Society Newsletter, Volume 18, Issue 1, January/February 1979.)

What happens on the inner planes is also later manifested on the mento-physical realms.

Starting early in 1980, the author began to be recognized for his humanitarian work by Orders of Chivalry from different parts of the world. In a short time the author became a highly respected and much decorated individual as recognition poured in from Princes and Grand Masters of Orders of Chivalry on Earth.

H.R. & I.H.Prince Henri III Paleologue bestowed the title of Count de Florina on Sir George King in the summer of 1980 and he was subsequently crowned at an official Coronation held in America on May 31st, 1981. Previous to this in 1980, he received from France the much coveted "l'Etoile de la Paix", only a few of which have ever been given.

Soon after this, on August 23rd, 1980, His Excellency Count George King de Florina was anointed, consecrated, appointed and created an Archbishop in the presence of two more Archbishops and a Bishop in New York. He was instructed to "Go forth and found your own Religion."

Although The Aetherius Society had been in existence for 25 years prior to this, by ecclesiastical law, the release enabled Count George King de Florina to become His Eminence Metropolitan Archbishop of The Aetherius Churches. This title was soon recognized by other Archbishops from France who bestowed further honours upon His Eminence. Count George King's name also appears in the "1981

Directory of Distinguished Americans" and the book of European nobility. His Eminence Count George King was also nominated as "Minister of the Year for 1981" by the Board of Directors of the International Evangelism Crusades — a worldwide religious denomination of Ministers in 49 different countries.

Further Knighthoods were bestowed upon Count George King by prominent Orders of Chivalry. He was given high positions in some of these Orders.

His work for the Republic of Poland in exile was also recognized by prominent government officials.

On Thursday, April 16th, 1981, a most unusual Transmission was delivered by a Cosmic Master Who uses the pseudonym — Mars Sector 6. This Cosmic Master has, throughout the years, delivered many great Transmissions of profound wisdom to Earth. The Society has published some of these. (Note 1.) During this most unusual Transmission, the first of its kind ever given in the 27 years of previous communication, the following statement was made by the Cosmic Master:

"The Academy Of Space Sciences have made the following Awards of Merit and Honour to George King for the invention and performance of 'Operation Sunbeam':
Saturn Peace Prize for Humanities;
Venus Peace Prize for Humanities;
The Mars Sector 6 Peace Prize for Humanities;
Ruby Medal Of Honour, and two Stars, for Valour." (Note 2.)

And thus was the author greatly honoured by the elevated Cosmic Beings for the outstanding design and performance of the Karmic manipulation on behalf of mankind termed "Operation Sunbeam", which had been running successfully for several years.

On July 19th, 1981, before a large and distinguished gathering in the Dorchester Hotel, Park Lane, London, His Highness Prince Pensavalle, President of the International Union of Christian Chivalry, gave the much coveted "Prize of Peace and Justice" to His Eminence in recognition for his tireless work and charity to humanity. As a further great compliment, H.H. Prince Pensavalle flew in specially from Rome to give this award. It should be remembered that this Peace Prize is only given very rarely and then only after rigorous enquiries made by the President and the Grand Council. The Peace

Prize has, in the past, been given to such people as Professor Einstein, Mother Theresa of Calcutta, Dr. Henry Kissinger and Dr. Albert Schweitzer.

On Saturday, September 26th, 1981, the Coronation of Their Serene Highnesses Prince George King and Princess Monique King de Santorini was performed by H.R. & I.H. Prince Henri III Paleologue at St. George's Church, Hanover Square, London. This Coronation was performed according to the rules of ancient tradition.

Soon after being crowned as His Serene Highness Prince George King de Santorini by H.R. & I.H. Prince Henri III Paleologue representing one of the oldest noble houses on Earth today, Prince George King founded an Order of Chivalry known as "The Mystical Order of Saint Peter." H.R. & I.H. consented, in deference to Prince George, to become the Eminent Royal Protector of this Order, and to extend, through the Prince Grand Master, his "Fons Honorum" (Fountain of Honour) thereby making this Order of Chivalry high among the most legitimate Orders on Earth today.

Thus, in only two years after the initial Ceremony of Knighthood held on Shamballa, H.S.H. Prince George King was given the highest honours which are possible to give to any man who was not born of noble birth.

Indeed there was a Master Plan at work which inspired people in position to recognize the devotion of an individual and to come forward most boldly with this recognition.

These are some of the many high honours which were bestowed upon the Founder President of The Aetherius Society by great people who had come to recognize His Eminence for what he was — a man completely dedicated to God and to the salvation of humanity.

Years before this, he had been recognized, carefully analyzed and later chosen by Cosmic Forces as, "Primary Terrestrial Mental Channel" and it is in the capacity of "Primary Terrestrial Mental Channel" that he writes this book, "Operation Space Magic — The Cosmic Connection."

FOREWORD

This book, "Operation Space Magic — The Cosmic Connection", is written in such a way as to give the reader relevant information which can be understood quite easily. As "Operation Space Magic" was, because of its very nature, an extremely complex undertaking, the author decided to give the information regarding the Operation, as brief, terse answers to numerous questions. The Log Sheets appearing herein were devised by the author, with the help of Dr. Michael Scholey, a Spiritual Energy Radiator Initiate from the American Headquarters of The Aetherius Society. Dr. Michael Scholey deserves the thanks and recognition from the Publishers for his valuable help to the author in this respect.

The information to the specially devised questions is given by the author who has been commissioned by The Supreme Hierarchal Council of this Solar System on the Planet Saturn, to reveal this information regarding "Operation Space Magic."

This book gives a description of a Space Action performed by Beings referred to simply as — The Six Adepts. The Six Adepts are Interplanetary Intelligences Who live on the physical and subtle realms of the Planet Earth. Three of These, Whose true identity is not revealed, but referred to under the code names of Nixies Zero Zero One, Nixies Zero Zero Two and Nixies Zero Zero Three, inhabit terrestrial bodies and were born into the life form system of Earth in a way somewhat similar to an ordinary terrestrial birth, in that They inhabit a normal carbon-based cellular structure. The other two Adepts, namely, Nixies Zero Zero Four and Nixies Zero Zero Five, do not inhabit a base physical structure and because of this, are less limited in Their action and capabilities than Their three Colleagues. However, all of The Five Adepts are operating under a limitation imposed upon Them by the Divine Law of Karma, in that only a fraction of Their full consciousness is contained within Their physical and auric structures. This part of Their consciousness is referred to as — the fourth aspect.

Nixies Zero Zero Six is in a quite different Karmic position. The identity of this Interplanetary Intelligence is known by The Spiritual Hierarchy Of Earth in that He, as The Lord Babaji, is the political and Spiritual Head of The Spiritual Hierarchy Of Earth. Although not operating in full consciousness while on Earth, The Lord Babaji does inhabit an Ascended body which is ageless in that, folklore and occult investigation would seem to suggest that He has been on Earth for thousands of years and has decided to remain on Earth until His services are no longer required.

These Six Adepts have performed outstanding deeds for the benefit and protection of mankind throughout Their lifetimes, and although the true identities of five of Them remain strictly classified, They work in various ways, tirelessly, in order to help the human race on the Planet Earth.

More information regarding the unparalleled deeds performed by The Six Adepts for all life forms on Earth, whether mineral, vegetable or sentient, can be gained by a study of Aetherius Society literature. (Note 3.)

Regarding "Operation Space Magic", an official communique was delivered publicly by the author on January 25th, 1981, and later published in The Aetherius Society Journal called "Cosmic Voice." This official communique ran as follows:

"By the power vested in me by The Cosmic Masters, under the title and responsibility of 'Primary Terrestrial Mental Channel', and for the good of all terrestrial life, it is my privilege and deep honour to be granted the permission to issue the following communique on behalf of The Six Adepts, operating under the instructions and authority of The Supreme Council of the Solar System based upon Saturn:

"The Cosmic Connection of 'Operation Space Magic' was successfully concluded on January 23rd, 1981, between the hours of 2:35 p.m. and 3:55 p.m. Pacific Standard Time, by The Six Adepts Who placed a complex Satellite in orbit of this Earth. This Satellite was designed and prepared to have an orbital and operating expectancy of over 1,000 terrene years.

"This Satellite has the capability, when correctly coded by Interplanetary Personnel, to receive high frequencies of Spiritual Energies from the Planets Saturn, Jupiter, Venus and Neptune. These Spiritual Energies can then be collected, in a controlled manner, by the Masters from Gotha and other Cosmic Intelligences Who have gained permission, and transmitted to The Ineffable Logos Of Terra through 'Operation Sunbeam' equipment operated by The Aetherius Society as well as The Spiritual Hierarchy Of Earth, through carefully charted

Psychic Centres in the Body of the Planet Earth, in order to bring about an essential stabilization of internal and external conditions on this Planet.

"This official communique is issued by:

> His Eminence, Count Doctor George King de Florina, Metropolitan Archbishop of The Aetherius Churches;
> With the Sanction and Authority of The Supreme Council of the Solar System based on Saturn;
> With the Sanction and Authority of The Protectors Of The Flame Of The Ineffable Logos Of Terra;
> With the Sanction and Authority of The Six Adepts."

After the publication of this scientific treatise, His Eminence has agreed to hold specialized Seminars for a more complete study of the implications and modus operandi of this complex, far-reaching inner and outer Space project. His Eminence is prepared to reveal as much information regarding this Space project, which was conducted by The Six Adepts on behalf of all life upon this Planet Earth, as he is allowed to do by Higher Authority.

This book, then, is a terse statement of basic scientific facts, produced in an easily understandable manner for the public, of one of the most ambitious Space projects undertaken by The Six Adepts to date on behalf of all life upon the Planet Terra.

AUTHOR'S RECOMMENDATIONS

NOTE 1.   Study of the profound Teachings delivered by the Cosmic Master, Mars Sector 6 is highly recommended to all New Age students.

See the following books: *The Nine Freedoms; The Day The Gods Came; You Are Responsible!; Wisdom Of The Planets; Life On The Planets; Cosmic Voice Volume 1; Cosmic Voice,* Issues 22-26; *Join Your Ship; A Cosmic Message Of Divine Opportunity.*

The following Metacassettes® contain Transmissions from this Cosmic Master recorded as they were delivered: MC-9, *Power Transmissions For Members;* MC-10, *Watcher In The Night;* MC-12, *Operation Prayer Power — A Spiritual Dream Come True;* MC-14, *Ye Are Gods;* MC-15, *From Freewill To Freedom;* MC-16, *Action Is Essential;* MC-17, *Fight Ye The Evil;* MC-18, *Be Sane Ye Men.*

NOTE 2.   For the full text of the amazing Transmission from Cosmic Sources, see *Cosmic Voice,* Volume 2, Issues 7 & 8, May 1981.

NOTE 3.   For many years, The Adepts have dedicated Their unique skills and abilities to the service of this world. Through The Aetherius Society mankind has a record of the vital Mission of protection undertaken by these Great Beings, as well as Their cooperation with, and participation in Spiritual Missions of immense benefit to all life on Earth.

The primary reason for the presence of The Five Adepts on Earth at this time in man's history, is to protect life on Earth from the powers of darkness in the lower astral realms and to bring about the transmutation of the worst evil in these realms. For a study of this vital Service to humanity, read *The Three Saviours Are Here!* written by the author. The Transmission of the same title is available on Metacassette® No. MC-25.

Cassette No. C-55, *The Men Who Won Operation Karmalight For You,* demonstrates the tremendous limitations and difficulties under which The Adepts had to operate in an horrendous conflict against the ruler of the hells. A fuller account of this Mission, "Operation Karmalight", one of the most important to the salvation of humanity in its entire history on this Earth, appears in The Aetherius Society Newsletter, Volume 6, Issue 22, November 1967 through Volume 7, Issue 24, November 1968; and Volume 8, Issues 1 & 2, January 1969 through Issues 8-10, April/May 1969.

Further Missions of protection of The Adepts include *The World Emergency*, during which alien intelligences unintentionally presented a dangerous threat to life on Earth. See The Aetherius Society Newsletter, Volume 11, Issue 14, October 1972 and Volume 12, Issues 1-3, January/February 1973. Also read *The Atomic Mission* which describes a dangerous action undertaken by The Adepts to neutralize a world-threatening radio-active mutation on the lower astral realms of Earth.

During special Stand-By periods, The Adepts (and the author) help to hold the balance of Karma for humanity during the absence of Masters from The Spiritual Hierarchy Of Earth for Initiatory purposes. Study of *A Special Assignment,* and Metacassette® No. MC-10 *Watcher In The Night,* will provide a greater understanding of these important times.

An account of the participation of The Adepts in "Operation Sunbeam" can be read in The Aetherius Society Newsletter, Volume 15, Issues 20-22, November 1976, when 21 special Phases of this Mission were performed. The Adepts have also been very active in the Cosmic Mission, "Operation Prayer Power." Designed by the author, this Mission enables Prayer Energy, invoked by ordinary people, to be stored for potent release, when needed, to a stricken area of the world. The Adepts have been instrumental in manipulating this Prayer Energy, when released, often with miraculous results, and have also helped in the collection of Spiritual Energy for this Mission. See *The Aetherius Society Newsletter,* Volume 13, Issues 16-20, August/September 1974; *Cosmic Voice,* Volume 1, Issues 5-8, October/November 1980, and Volume 2, Issues 2 & 3, February 1981; *Cosmic Voice,* Volume 2, Issues 10-12, August/September 1981.

All references to books and cassettes given above are available from the Publishers, The Aetherius Society.

OPERATION SPACE MAGIC
THE COSMIC CONNECTION

VEHICLE DATA

Type: Long Range Interceptor Craft.

Classification: Combat.

Designed by: The Perfects of Saturn.

Manufactured by: Martian Technicians.

Number: Coded symbols — not translatable into English.

Commissioning date: January 22nd, 1979.

Commissioning Authority: The Supreme Council on Saturn.

Overruling Authority: The Supreme Council on Saturn.

VEHICLE SPECIFICATIONS

Physical characteristics:

(a) *Shape:* Circular disc aeroform with domed cabin.

(b) *Size:* 212 feet in diameter.

(c) *Specialized performance characteristics:*
Capable of velocities above C^{10} in certain vibrational sequences (Realms);
Drive system is capable of generating its own propulsive energy independent of any external re-energizing equipment;
Life support systems have a limited capacity and need base or Spacecraft Carrier for recharging.

(d) *Maximum Personnel capacity:* 15+.

(e) *Maximum cargo capacity:* Not known.

(f) *Range:* Classified — I.C. (Interplanetary Confederation) Code 11/11.

(g) *Hull Material — List briefly:*   Self-regenerating cellular metal.

VEHICLE SYSTEMS

Propulsion units:

(a) *Primary:*   Classified — I.C. Code 11/11.

(b) *Secondary:*   Uses magnetic, gravitational and reactory lines of force through Space which are controllable by on-board equipment.

(c) *Back-up to primary and secondary:*   Ion drive with discriminatory capabilities to lock into either:

   1) two pole gravitation, or

   2) existing magnetic lines of force caused by Planetary movement and/or perturbations of mass in Space.

(d) *Emergency:*   In any Solar System, is capable of differentiation and control of gravitational forces.

(e) *Any unusual capabilities:*   This specific type of craft is capable of coming to a complete cessation of all movement. Thereby — under such conditions — is capable of a limited Time Control. (Note 1.)

Navigational systems:

(a) *Primary:* A sophisticated cosmotronic computer capable of detecting, by beam transmission, the exact velocity of bodies moving through Space and their relative position to other bodies moving through Space. This produces a five-point coordination with reference to these bodies, with millisecond recalculated position updates;
   Intergalactic navigational capabilities with unspecified limitation: Classified — I.C. Code 11/11.

(b) *Secondary:*   Same as primary, but with a limited range focus.

(c) *Back-up to primary and secondary:*   Within a Solar System, beam transmission capable of measuring the exact velocity of a

Sun and Its relationship to other Planets in a Solar System, with 5- to 12-point coordinated reference, with millisecond update.

(d) <u>Emergency:</u> All systems have similar back-up systems and these can be used under all known applicable conditions.

Communication systems:
All ranges. Two-channel cosmotronic beam carrying cosmotronically amplified thought impulses;
Uses plug-in crystal recordings containing known communication codes with possible Aliens. (Note 2.)

Detector apparatus:
Two-way cosmotronic beam revolved in a 360-degree arc around craft. Used for all ranges of detection, from short to ultra long range. Capable of differentiation between sentient life forms and non-sentient life forms. (Note 3.)

Armament:

(<u>Note:</u> If armament still on I.C. Classified List, list I.C. Classification Codes.)

(a) *Main armament fixed to vessel structure:*
Modified "nirron" projectors capable of causing a vibrational sequence through which the particles making up an atomic structure are brought into close proximity, thereby causing molecular and atomic change within the structure. All "empty" space is removed from around the atomic particles. This weapon cannot be used until activated by the Overruling Authority.

(b) *Secondary armament fixed to vessel structure:*
Short range sonic beam capable of rendering sentient beings insensible. This can also disrupt electronic or cosmotronic circuitry in robots.

(c) *Primary self-propelled armament:*
Apparatus capable of launching long, medium and short range computer guided torpedoes containing "anti-matter" explosives.

(d) *Secondary self-propelled armament:*
Sonic torpedoes capable of rendering local insensibility to sen-

tient beings or disruption of electronic or cosmotronic circuitry in robots. (Armament Classified I.C. Code 11/11.)

Protective screening:

(*a*) <u>Primary</u>: Force screen capable of enclosing the entire craft.

(*b*) <u>Secondary:</u> Projectile launchers capable of disrupting any external communication from hostile craft, from cosmotronic to pure unassisted telepathy;
Screen of invisibility caused by the rotation of photons in a 360-degree arc around vessel.

(*c*) <u>Emergency:</u> Short range projectile launchers which disintegrate, causing reactions producing temperatures of 6,000 degrees C. + into force screens of hostiles;
All systems have the minimum of three completely isolated back-up circuits.

If Vehicle is of specialized combat type, state method of Personnel acceptance by Overruling Authority:

By analytical organ print computer under remote control of Overruling Authority. The computer measures and analyzes the entire physical and neurological structure of the subject, using a specialized fluid which, after drinking, pervades and penetrates all areas of the physical and nervous structure. The computer analysis must correspond with the original analysis held on file by the Overruling Authority.

If this internal organ print is not verified by the Overruling Authority, then the subject is immobilized with a restraining screen until further investigation takes place. This computerized equipment is so finely tuned that not even a clone replica of the original authorized Entity would be accepted as legitimate.

This equipment cannot be changed or adjusted except by the Overruling Authority. Any unauthorized attempt to do so could render the interfering entity insensible or could even prove fatal to the interfering entity.

These strict rules apply to all craft under I.C. jurisdiction or influence: they do not necessarily apply to alien craft not under I.C. jurisdiction or influence.

Other specialized equipment:

1) This is strictly classified — I.C. Code 11/11.

2) This craft can be totally destroyed in six different ways:

    a) at any distance by the Overruling Authority, or

    b) by authorized Personnel, either from inside or at a distance from the craft.

VEHICLE OPERATIONAL PERSONNEL

Normal operational conditions:

Minimum number: Six.

Categories: Captain.
Chief Navcom Officer
Second Navcom Officer
Computer Officer
Armaments Officer
Tractor Beam Officer

Combat conditions:

Minimum number: Ten.

Categories: Captain
Co-Pilot
Chief Navcom Officer
Second Navcom Officer
Chief Computer Officer
Second Computer Officer
Chief Armaments Officer
Second Armaments Officer
Telepathic Advisory Officer
Tractor Beam Officer

Give latest ranks of operating Personnel (I.C. Classification only):

Nixies Zero Zero One:
    Rank — Commander.
    Acting Rank — Vice Admiral.

Nixies Zero Zero Two:
    Rank — Commander.
    Acting Rank — Vice Admiral.

Nixies Zero Zero Three:
    Rank — Commander.
    Acting Rank — Vice Admiral.

Nixies Zero Zero Four:
    Acting Rank — Commander.
    When necessary — Rear Admiral or Vice Admiral.

Nixies Zero Zero Five:
    Rank — Commander.
    Acting Rank — Vice Admiral or Rear Admiral.

Nixies Zero Zero Six:
    In Space, Acting Rank — Commander.
    Acting Rank — Vice Admiral or Rear Admiral.

SPECIAL INSTRUCTION:
If vehicle is a combat type vessel operating under Closed Authority, it is necessary for all Personnel to be capable of operating, navigating and landing vehicle in case of emergency. (Note 4.)

Is this understood: Yes.

AUTHOR'S RECOMMENDATIONS

NOTE 1.　In simple terminology, this means that by using tremendous forces, understood only by the original Designers, this craft is able to be controlled for a limited period so that all change, for this period, takes place outside of the craft. This produces a manipulation, or "time warp", whereby the craft exists as a stationary entity, allowing time to produce change outside of its existence.

NOTE 2.　If these craft are operating in an alien Galaxy, when released from a Spacecraft Carrier, they would be equipped with communication codes for identification and communication with all known aliens likely to be encountered in that part of that particular Galaxy.

NOTE 3.　As everything is living with differing degrees of intelligence coefficients, then the reference made here to "non-sentient life forms", applies to robots, metals, crystals, vegetation, etc.

The detector apparatus consists of a Saturnian Analyzer which projects two crystal-locked beams of energy — one inside the other. The outer beam acts as a carrier for the inner returning echo. When subjected to specialized computer analysis, molecular, atomic and sub-atomic construction of any known mass can be determined.

The Saturnian Analyzer is also capable of assessing the degree of intelligence displayed by Sentient Beings by measuring and evaluating the mental energy output resulting from any stimuli.

The Saturnian Analyzer operates over long, medium and short ranges.

This apparatus is also available in a portable unit which can be worn and used by an Interplanetary Intelligence Who has been personally Initiated by The Perfects Of Saturn.

NOTE 4.　Although the Interceptor Craft used by The Six Adepts in this Mission was a combat vessel, by far the most frequent use of this Spacecraft is search-and-rescue. This craft can be modified for tactical search-and-rescue operations or for decontamination operations on a large scale.

In the search-and-rescue mode, the Spacecraft is equipped with a fully self-contained operating theatre. Operations on a physical or auric structure can be undertaken. Cosmotronic, radionic, sonic and chromotherapeutical healing techniques can also be undertaken while the Spacecraft is either in flight or stationary.

This craft is also capable of carrying long, medium or short range cosmotronically guided torpedoes which can be launched and guided with great accuracy for the decontamination of any body of Space, irrespective of its size and gravitational mass, or any spore field which, because of a threatened danger to Sentient Beings, demands either destruction or re-guidance into another position of Space.

****

TYPICAL I.C. SPACECRAFT

An illustration of a model of a Spacecraft made from information obtained from several reliable sources by the author. Although not an exact replica of the latest Long Range Interceptor Craft used by The Six Adepts in the Missions reported herein, it does convey a general idea of the basic external characteristics of the aeroform.

OPERATIONAL PHASE LOG
- PHASE ONE -

Operation Name: SPACE MAGIC.

Phase number: One.

Date: March 5, 1980; Earth Year 16.242. (Note 1.)

Nature of Operation: Placement of remote module tuned to Satellite in orbit of Terra.

Operational destination: Saturn.

Authorizing Authority(s): The Supreme Council on Saturn; The Interplanetary Confederation; The Protectors Of The Ineffable Flame Of The Logos Of Terra.

Date of authorization: Early 1975; Earth Year 11.

Authorization applied for by — (I.C. Code Names only): (Note 2.)
Nixies Zero Zero One;
Nixies Zero Zero Two;
Nixies Zero Zero Three;
Nixies Zero Zero Four;
Nixies Zero Zero Five;
Nixies Zero Zero Six.
(All in Full Aspect.)

Estimated time for this Operation to be in effect:
1,000 + terrene years.

Position and Authority of annalist:
Primary Terrestrial Mental Channel, reference I.C. Authorization.

OPERATIONAL DATA

Operation Personnel by rank and name (*I.C. Code Names only*):
Captain — Nixies Zero Zero One
Chief Navcom Officer — Nixies Zero Zero Two
Second Navcom Officer — Nixies Zero Zero Four
Computer Officers — Nixies Zero Zero Five and
— Nixies Zero Zero Two
Armaments Officer — Nixies Zero Zero Three
Cargo and Tractor Beam Officer — Nixies Zero Zero Six

Other Personnel: None.

VEHICLE USE

Vehicle type: Long Range Interceptor Craft.

Distance covered: 1,573.6 million miles.(Note 3.)

Peak velocity used: Classified I.C. Code 11/11.
Level 4 "hyperspace projection." (Note 4.)

Was remote control used: Yes.

If affirmative, how far from destination was remote activated:
Nine million miles.

Was landing escort provided from destination: Yes.

If affirmative, how many vehicles in escort (*state type*): Five:
Four Long Range Interceptor Craft;
One small Spacecraft Carrier.

Did vehicle land: Yes.

If affirmative, give reason for landing: To affix module into surface of Planet.

Position of landing (*give coordinates*): Strictly classified — I.C. Code 11/11.

Landing procedure (state briefly): The Interceptor Craft was guided into the landing by Saturn Control which locked into the craft computer banks at a distance of nine million miles from destination.

Was armament used: Yes.

If affirmative, was this for defense: No.

If not defensive, state purpose: To drill four pylon holes to affix module structure into foundation.

Was help given to Operations Force by Surface Intelligences:
Yes, help offered.

If affirmative, how many Intelligences were involved: Five.

If affirmative, were they Sentient Beings or robots: Sentient Beings.

If Sentient, were They in projected state, Full Aspect or other aspect: Full Aspect.

Was protective screening used: Yes.

If affirmative, for what reason: As a protection from severe cosmic ray bombardment, low temperatures and atmospheric pressure.

Was a module or other device left on surface: Yes, one.

If affirmative, state whether active or passive: Active.

If active, state energy source of module or device:
Solar energy batteries recharged from tracking solar panels; Magnetic energy from the Planet.

State weight of module or device: Classified — I.C. Code 11/11.

If module or device was left, state capabilities and functions:
To collect Universal Life Forces conditioned by the Planet Saturn and transmit these to a Satellite in orbit of Terra for further use in "Operation Sunbeam" and other Operations.

If module or device was left, is it self-charging: Yes.

If module or device was left, is it self-adjusting: Yes, within limits outlined below.

Does module or device need regular attention: Yes.

If affirmative, state periods between attention: Approximately 364 terrene days.

If affirmative, state nature of this attention: To fine tune solar energy receivers, fine tune magnetic energy receivers, check and adjust transmitter if necessary.

If affirmative, Who will attend to module or device: Technicians from Saturn.

If affirmative, was agreement made with Surface Authority for this attention: Yes.

EQUIPMENT EVALUATION

Did all vehicle equipment perform to specifications: Yes.

If negative, describe malfunction:

(a) *Mechanical:* None.

(b) *Cosmotronic:* None.

(c) *Radionic:* None.

Technicians' suggestion(s) (I.C. Coding acceptable): Not applicable.

Authority to which malfunction was reported: Not applicable.

How was this malfunction reported:

(a) *By cosmotronic means:* Not applicable.

(b) *By telepathic means:* Not applicable.

(c) *By other means:* Not applicable.

How soon after discovery of malfunction was report made:
  Not applicable.

If any appreciable time-lag before reporting, give reason(s) for this:
  Not applicable.

Was confirmation of receipt of malfunction report received from reporting Authority: Not applicable.

How soon after malfunction report was confirmation received:
  Not applicable.

How was confirmation transmitted:

(a) *By cosmotronic means:* Not applicable.

(b) *By telepathic means:* Not applicable.

(c) *By other means:* Not applicable.

PERSONAL PROTECTION DEVICE EVALUATION

Conditions under which personal protection device was worn:

(a) *In free Space:* By Nixies Zero Zero One, Nixies Zero Zero Two, Nixies Zero Zero Three and Nixies Zero Zero Six, immediately after projection until entry into Spacecraft.

(b) *On Planetary body:* By all Personnel.

If Planetary body, list:

  Atmospheric temperature: Minus 243 degrees F. (Note 5.)

  Surface gravity (use Terra as 1.0): 1.18.

Was full Space armour needed: Yes.

Was full Space armour worn: Yes.

If negative, state what other protective garment worn: Type:
  Not applicable.

Under conditions worn, how was overall performance of suit:
Excellent.

If very low temperatures were experienced, how long would heating elements and life support systems have performed:

Excellently: Approximately 10 terrene hours.

Barely adequately: Approximately 12 terrene hours.

If very high temperatures were experienced, how long would cooling elements and life support systems have performed:

Excellently: Not applicable.

Barely adequately: Not applicable.

How long was suit in use: Approximately 20-30 terrene minutes.
(*Special Note: Do not take into account possible recharging and refueling of life support systems in the above answers.*)

Was recharging and/or refueling of life support systems feasible under Operation conditions: Yes.

How well did suit protect from cosmic ray bombardment:
Excellently.

Was suit equipped with an anti-gravity device: Yes.

If affirmative, how was its performance: Excellent.

How well did the suit's internal negative-ion discharge generator work: Excellently.

PERSONNEL EVALUATION

Was projection from terrestrial counterparts necessary for this flight: Yes.

If affirmative, Who projected (I.C. Code Names only):
Nixies Zero Zero One;

Nixies Zero Zero Two;
Nixies Zero Zero Three;
Nixies Zero Zero Six.

PROJECTION DATA ON: Nixies Zero Zero One.

(a) *Time preparation commenced:* 14:00 hours Pacific Standard Time, March 5, 1980 — Earth Year 16.242.

(b) *Time of division (projection):* 14:15 hours P.S.T. (Note 6.)

(c) *If projecting from fourth aspect, list difficulties encountered to make up to Full Aspect:*
Detachment from surroundings;
Rise of Kundalini, especially if Adept in depleted physical condition;
Charging and de-charging of lower Psychic Centres.

(d) *Time of return to fourth aspect:* 15:21 hours P.S.T.

(e) *List difficulties encountered in returning to fourth aspect:*
Detachment from Full Aspect of a part of the consciousness and re-attachment of this part of the consciousness to a base physical structure which has been inactive for a certain time, causes extreme coldness and severe neuro-physical strain.

PROJECTION DATA ON: Nixies Zero Zero Two.

(a) *Time preparation commenced:* 13:50 hours P.S.T., March 5, 1980 — Earth Year 16.242.

(b) *Time of division (projection):* 14:15 hours P.S.T.

(c) *If projecting from fourth aspect, list difficulties encountered to make up to Full Aspect:*
Detachment from surroundings;
Rise of Kundalini, especially if Adept in depleted physical condition;
Charging and de-charging of lower Psychic Centres.

(d) *Time of return to fourth aspect:* 15:21 hours P.S.T.

(e) *List difficulties encountered in returning to fourth aspect:*
   Detachment from Full Aspect of a part of the consciousness and re-attachment of this part of the consciousness to a base physical structure which has been inactive for a certain time, causes extreme coldness and severe neuro-physical strain.

PROJECTION DATA ON: Nixies Zero Zero Three.

(a) *Time preparation commenced:* 13:45 hours P.S.T., March 5, 1980 — Earth Year 16.242.

(b) *Time of division (projection):* 14:15 hours P.S.T.

(c) *If projecting from fourth aspect, list difficulties encountered to make up to Full Aspect:*
   Detachment from surroundings;
   Rise of Kundalini, especially if Adept in depleted physical condition;
   Charging and de-charging of lower Psychic Centres.

(d) *Time of return to fourth aspect:* 15:21 hours P.S.T.

(e) *List difficulties encountered in returning to fourth aspect:*
   Detachment from Full Aspect of a part of the consciousness and re-attachment of this part of the consciousness to a base physical structure which has been inactive for a certain time, causes extreme coldness and severe neuro-physical strain.

PROJECTION DATA ON: Nixies Zero Zero Six.

(a) *Time preparation commenced:* 14:00 hours P.S.T., March 5, 1980 — Earth Year 16.242.

(b) *Time of division (projection):* 14:15 hours P.S.T.

(c) *If projecting from fourth aspect, list difficulties encountered to make up to Full Aspect:*
   Detachment from surroundings;
   Rise of Kundalini, especially if Adept in depleted physical condition;
   Charging and de-charging of lower Psychic Centres.

(*d*) *Time of return to fourth aspect:* 15:21 hours P.S.T.

(*e*) *List difficulties encountered in returning to fourth aspect:*
Detachment from Full Aspect of a part of the consciousness and re-attachment of this part of the consciousness to a base physical structure which has been inactive for a certain time, causes extreme coldness and severe neuro-physical strain.

Where did Projected Forms pick up operational vehicle:

(*a*) *At a predetermined destination with a static vehicle:* No.

(*b*) *With vehicle in flight:* Yes.

(*c*) *If (b) affirmative, how far was projection from physical body to vehicle:* Between 100,000 miles and 200,000 miles.

(*d*) *If (b) affirmative, state reason(s) why this was done:*
In order to protect the terrene Level One physical structure by reducing the time out of the terrene Level One physical body.

Were there any injuries to Sentient Beings in this flight: No.

If affirmative, when was injury(s) noticed: Not applicable.

If affirmative, give full particulars of injury(s), no matter how minor:
Not applicable.

If affirmative, state reason(s) as to cause of injury(s):
Not applicable.

What measures were taken to rectify this:

(*a*) *At time noticed:* Not applicable.

(*b*) *In future operations:* Not applicable.

When was injury(s) treated: Not applicable.

Where was injury(s) treated: Not applicable.

Was this injury(s) reported to a Higher Authority: Not applicable.

How was this injury(s) reported:

(a) *By cosmotronic means:*   Not applicable.

(b) *By telepathic means:*   Not applicable.

(c) *By other means:*   Not applicable.

How soon after discovery of injury(s) was report made:
   Not applicable.

If any appreciable time-lag before reporting, give reason(s) for this:
   Not applicable.

Was confirmation of receipt of injury(s) report received from reporting Authority: Not applicable.

How soon after injury(s) report was confirmation received:
   Not applicable.

How was confirmation transmitted:

(a) *By cosmotronic means:*   Not applicable.

(b) *By telepathic means:*   Not applicable.

(c) *By other means:*   Not applicable.

AUTHOR'S RECOMMENDATIONS

NOTE 1.   In 1979 the author was notified that the Masters on Level Six had decided to reorganize the calendar and henceforth, the new calendar would be dated from July 8th, 1964, the most significant date on this Earth. July 8th, 1964 therefore becomes Earth Year 1, Earth Day 1, written as: E.Y. 1.1. — the years changing every July 8th and the days going up to 365 (except leap years, which are 366).

July 8th, 1964 marks "The Primary Initiation Of Earth" when this Planet received stupendous Initiatory Energies which, as released, will, in a gradual and controlled manner, raise the Earth onto a higher Spiritual plane. This Initiation will result in the much-prophesied New Age for both the Planet Herself and those upon Her who are ready. The only report of this most important event in history is written up by the author in a book entitled *The Day The Gods Came,* obtainable from The Aetherius Society.

NOTE 2.   "I.C. Code Names only" means the code names of individuals as appearing in the records of The Interplanetary Confederation.

NOTE 3.   The distance to each of the Planets referred to is given in figures based on terrestrial astronomical calculations at that time. True and precise distances remain classified.

NOTE 4.   The Interceptor Craft used by The Adepts on the first Four Phases of this operation, was capable of travel in another vibratory sequence (realms) above the normally accepted Level One (base physical realms).

All journeys to and from Planets during this operation were made on Level Four and, therefore, vast distances could be covered in a very short time period without the usual dangers which would be encountered if the same velocities had been used on the basic physical realms.

Different physical and Spiritual laws apply to what the author has termed "hyperspace projection."

The peak velocity known in the Universe has been described by a

Cosmic Master thus: *"A point of consciousness under Karmic direction attains the ultimate velocity in Creation."* (See The Aetherius Society Newsletter Volume 11, Issues 9 & 10, July 1972.)

It must be remembered that the high level Authority given to The Six Adepts in Full Aspect by Saturn High Command would also constitute a Karmic Decree. This is probably the reason why an I.C. classification has been put on all peak velocities used in "Operation Space Magic."

NOTE 5. The surface temperatures and gravities reported throughout the text are terrestrial opinions of these phenomena, rather than exact recordings taken by The Adepts on the Planets visited.

The temperature of 500 degrees Fahrenheit reported here as a possible surface temperature on Venus is a modification of terrestrial scientific findings, and is not claimed to be the exact temperature measured in the particular geographical position of the surface visited by The Adepts.

For some reason best known to the Overruling Authority, the exact temperatures and surface gravities of these Planets were not released.

NOTE 6. P.S.T. stands for Pacific Standard Time.

OPERATIONAL PHASE LOG
- PHASE TWO -

Operation Name: SPACE MAGIC.

Phase number: Two.

Date: March 6, 1980; Earth Year 16.243.

Nature of Operation: Placement of remote module tuned to Satellite in orbit of Terra.

Operation destination: Jupiter.

Authorizing Authority(s): The Supreme Council on Saturn;
The Interplanetary Confederation;
The Protectors Of The Ineffable Flame Of The Logos Of Terra.

Date of authorization: Early 1975; Earth Year 11.

Authorization applied for by — (I.C. Code Names only):
Nixies Zero Zero One;
Nixies Zero Zero Two;
Nixies Zero Zero Three;
Nixies Zero Zero Four;
Nixies Zero Zero Five;
Nixies Zero Zero Six.
(All in Full Aspect).

Estimated time for this Operation to be in effect:
1,000 + terrene years.

Position and Authority of annalist:
Primary Terrestrial Mental Channel, reference I.C. Authorization.

OPERATIONAL DATA

Operational Personnel by rank and name (I.C. Code Names only):

Captain	— Nixies Zero Zero One
Chief Navcom Officer	— Nixies Zero Zero Two
Second Navcom Officer	— Nixies Zero Zero Four
Computer Officers	— Nixies Zero Zero Five and
	— Nixies Zero Zero Two
Armaments Officer	— Nixies Zero Zero Three
Cargo and Tractor Beam Officer	— Nixies Zero Zero Six

Other Personnel: None.

VEHICLE USE

Vehicle type: Long Range Interceptor Craft.

Distance covered: 821.7 million miles.

Peak velocity used: Classified I.C. Code 11/11.
Level 4 "hyperspace projection."

Was remote control used: Yes.

If affirmative, how far from destination was remote activated:
19 million miles.

Was landing escort provided from destination: Yes, from two million miles from destination.

If affirmative, how many vehicles in escort (state type): Four:
Three Long Range Interceptor Craft;
One small Spacecraft Carrier.

Did vehicle land: Yes.

If affirmative, give reason for landing: To affix module into surface of Planet.

Position of landing (give coordinates): Strictly classified — I.C. Code 11/11.

Landing procedure (state briefly):   The Interceptor Craft was guided into a landing by Jupiter Control which locked into the craft computer banks at a distance of 19 million miles from destination. Because of severe magnetic disturbance, causing ½ degree alignment error in approach pattern, a course correction had to be inserted into computer banks 10,000 miles from destination.

Was armament used: Yes.

If affirmative, was this for defense: No.

If not defensive, state purpose: To drill four pylon holes to affix module structure into foundation.

Was help given to Operations Force by Surface Intelligences:
   Yes, help offered.

If affirmative, how many Intelligences were involved: Three.

If affirmative, were they Sentient Beings or robots: Sentient Beings.

If Sentient, were They in projected state, Full Aspect or other aspect: Full Aspect.

Was protective screening used: Yes.

If affirmative, for what reason: As a protection from severe cosmic ray bombardment, low temperature and severe magnetic disturbance caused by Jupiterian Lunar orbits interacting with the orbits of 18 artificial Satellites orbiting Jupiter.

Was a module or other device left on surface: Yes, one.

If affirmative, state whether active or passive: Active.

If active, state energy source of module or device:
   Solar energy batteries, recharged from tracking solar panels; Magnetic energy from the Planet.

State weight of module or device: Classified — I.C. Code 11/11.

If module or device was left, state capabilities and functions:
   To collect Universal Life Forces conditioned by the Planet Jupiter

and transmit these to a Satellite in orbit of Terra for further use in "Operation Sunbeam" and other Operations.

If module or device was left, is it self-charging: Yes.

If module or device was left, is it self-adjusting: Yes, within limits outlined below.

Does module or device need regular attention: Yes.

If affirmative, state periods between attention: Approximately 364 terrene days.

If affirmative, state nature of this attention: To fine tune solar energy receivers, fine tune magnetic energy receivers, check and adjust transmitters if necessary.

If affirmative, Who will attend to module or device: Technicians from Jupiter.

If affirmative, was agreement made with Surface Authority for this attention: Yes.

EQUIPMENT EVALUATION

Did all vehicle equipment perform to specifications: Yes.

If negative, describe malfunction:

(a) *Mechanical:* None.

(b) *Cosmotronic:* None.

(c) *Radionic:* None.

Technicians' suggestion(s) (I.C. Coding acceptable): Not applicable.

Authority to which malfunction was reported: Not applicable.

How was this malfunction reported:

(a) *By cosmotronic means:* Not applicable.

(b) *By telepathic means:* Not applicable.

(c) *By other means:* Not applicable.

How soon after discovery of malfunction was report made:
Not applicable.

If any appreciable time-lag before reporting, give reason(s) for this:
Not applicable.

Was confirmation of receipt of malfunction report received from reporting Authority: Not applicable.

How soon after malfunction report was confirmation received:
Not applicable.

How was confirmation transmitted:

(a) *By cosmotronic means:* Not applicable.

(b) *By telepathic means:* Not applicable.

(c) *By other means:* Not applicable.

PERSONAL PROTECTION DEVICE EVALUATION

Conditions under which personal protection device was worn:

(a) *In free Space:* By Nixies Zero Zero One, Nixies Zero Zero Two, Nixies Zero Zero Three and Nixies Zero Zero Six, immediately after projection until entry into Spacecraft.

(b) *On Planetary body:* By all Personnel.

If Planetary body, list:

Atmospheric temperature: Minus 216 degrees F.

Surface gravity (use Terra as 1.0): 2.50.

Was full Space armour needed: Yes.

Was full Space armour worn: Yes.

If negative, state what other protective garment worn: Type:
  Not applicable.

Under conditions worn, how was overall performance of suit:
  Excellent.

If very low temperatures were experienced, how long would heating elements and life support systems have performed:

  Excellently: Approximately 10 terrene hours.

  Barely adequately: Approximately 12 terrene hours.

If very high temperatures were experienced, how long would cooling elements and life support systems have performed:

  Excellently: Not applicable.

  Barely adequately: Not applicable.

How long was suit in use: Approximately 20-30 terrene minutes.
  (Special Note: Do not take into account possible recharging and refueling of life support systems in the above answers.)

Was recharging and/or refueling of life support systems feasible under Operation conditions: Yes.

How well did suit protect from cosmic ray bombardment:
  Excellently.

Was suit equipped with an anti-gravity device: Yes.

If affirmative, how was its performance: Excellent.

How well did the suit's internal negative-ion discharge generator work: Excellently.

PERSONNEL EVALUATION

Was projection from terrestrial counterparts necessary for this flight: Yes.

If affirmative, Who projected (I.C. Code Names only):
   Nixies Zero Zero One;
   Nixies Zero Zero Two;
   Nixies Zero Zero Three;
   Nixies Zero Zero Six.

PROJECTION DATA ON: Nixies Zero Zero One.

(a) *Time preparation commenced:* 14:00 hours P.S.T., March 6, 1980 — Earth Year 16.243.

(b) *Time of division (projection):* 14.15 hours P.S.T.

(c) *If projecting from fourth aspect, list difficulties encountered to make up to Full Aspect:*
   Detachment from surroundings;
   Rise of Kundalini, especially if Adept in depleted physical condition;
   Charging and de-charging of lower Psychic Centres.

(d) *Time of return to fourth aspect:* 15.38 hours P.S.T.

(e) *List difficulties encountered in returning to fourth aspect:*
   Detachment from Full Aspect of a part of the consciousness and re-attachment of this part of the consciousness to a base physical structure which has been inactive for a certain time, causes extreme coldness and severe neuro-physical strain.

PROJECTION DATA ON: Nixies Zero Zero Two.

(a) *Time preparation commenced:* 13:50 hours P.S.T., March 6, 1980 — Earth Year 16.243.

(b) *Time of division (projection):* 14:15 hours P.S.T.

(c) *If projecting from fourth aspect, list difficulties encountered to make up to Full Aspect:*
   Detachment from surroundings;
   Rise of Kundalini, especially if Adept in depleted physical condition;
   Charging and de-charging of lower Psychic Centres.

(d) *Time of return to fourth aspect:* 15.38 hours P.S.T.

(e) *List difficulties encountered in returning to fourth aspect:*
   Detachment from Full Aspect of a part of the consciousness and re-attachment of this part of the consciousness to a base physical structure which has been inactive for a certain time, causes extreme coldness and severe neuro-physical strain.

PROJECTION DATA ON: Nixies Zero Zero Three.

(a) *Time preparation commenced:* 13:45 hours P.S.T., March 6, 1980 — Earth Year 16.243.

(b) *Time of division (projection):* 14:15 hours P.S.T.

(c) *If projecting from fourth aspect, list difficulties encountered to make up to Full Aspect:*
   Detachment from surroundings;
   Rise of Kundalini, especially if Adept in depleted physical condition;
   Charging and de-charging of lower Psychic Centres.

(d) *Time of return to fourth aspect:* 15:38 hours P.S.T.

(e) *List difficulties encountered in returning to fourth aspect:*
   Detachment from Full Aspect of a part of the consciousness and re-attachment of this part of the consciousness to a base physical structure which has been inactive for a certain time, causes extreme coldness and severe neuro-physical strain.

PROJECTION DATA ON: Nixies Zero Zero Six.

(a) *Time preparation commenced:* 14:00 hours P.S.T., March 6, 1980 — Earth Year 16.243.

(b) *Time of division (projection):* 14:15 hours P.S.T.

(c) *If projecting from fourth aspect, list difficulties encountered to make up to Full Aspect:*
   Detachment from surroundings;
   Rise of Kundalini, especially if Adept in depleted physical condition;

Charging and de-charging of lower Psychic Centres.

(d) *Time of return to fourth aspect:* 15:38 hours P.S.T.

(e) *List difficulties encountered in returning to fourth aspect:*
Detachment from Full Aspect of a part of the consciousness and re-attachment of this part of the consciousness to a base physical structure which has been inactive for a certain time, causes extreme coldness and severe neuro-physical strain.

Where did Projected Forms pick up operational vehicle:

(a) *At a predetermined destination with a static vehicle:* No.

(b) *With vehicle in flight:* Yes.

(c) *If (b) affirmative, how far was projection from physical body to vehicle:* Between 100,000 and 200,000 miles.

(d) *If (b) affirmative, state reason(s) why this was done:*
In order to protect the terrene Level One physical structure by reducing the time out of the terrene Level One physical body.

Were there any injuries to Sentient Beings on this flight:
Yes, to Nixies Zero Zero Two.

If affirmative, when was injury(s) noticed: After leaving surface of Jupiter.

If affirmative, give full particulars of injury(s), no matter how minor:
Adept was suffering from severe neuro-physical strain from which it could be diagnosed that this would have a grossly adverse effect upon the base physical body on His return to fourth aspect.

If affirmative, state reason(s) as to cause of injury(s):
Precipitated by an injury caused to fourth aspect in a previous engagement on lower levels of Terra.

What measures were taken to rectify this:

(a) *At time noticed:* Minor psychic surgery performed by Nixies Zero Zero Five, followed by auric stimulation.

(b) *In future Operations:* Whatever measures may be necessary or possible under operating conditions.

When was injury(s) treated: As soon as reported.

Where was injury(s) treated: In flight in Interceptor Craft.

Was this injury(s) reported to a Higher Authority: Yes.

How was this injury(s) reported:

(a) *By cosmotronic means:* Yes.

(b) *By telepathic means:* Yes.

(c) *By other means:* No.

How soon after discovery of injury(s) was report made: Immediately.

If any appreciable time-lag before reporting, give reason(s) for this: Not applicable.

Was confirmation of receipt of injury(s) report received from reporting Authority: Yes.

How soon after injury(s) report was confirmation received: 25-30 seconds.

How was confirmation transmitted:

(a) *By cosmotronic means:* Yes.

(b) *By telepathic means:* Yes.

(c) *By other means:* No.

OPERATIONAL PHASE LOG
- PHASE THREE -

Operation Name: SPACE MAGIC.

Phase number: Three.

Date: March 8, 1980; Earth Year 16.245.

Nature of Operation: Placement of one remote module and one booster station tuned to Satellite in orbit of Terra.

Operational destination: Venus.

Authorizing Authority(s): The Supreme Council on Saturn;
The Interplanetary Confederation;
The Protectors Of The Ineffable Flame Of The Logos Of Terra.

Date of authorization: Early 1975; Earth Year 11.

Authorization applied for by — (I.C. Code Names only):
Nixies Zero Zero One;
Nixies Zero Zero Two;
Nixies Zero Zero Three;
Nixies Zero Zero Four;
Nixies Zero Zero Five;
Nixies Zero Zero Six.
(All in Full Aspect.)

Estimated time for this Operation to be in effect:
1,000+ terrene years.

Position and Authority of annalist:
Primary Terrestrial Mental Channel, reference I.C. Authorization.

OPERATIONAL DATA

Operational Personnel by rank and name (I.C. Code Names only):

Captain	— Nixies Zero Zero One
Chief Navcom Officer	— Nixies Zero Zero Two
Second Navcom Officer	— Nixies Zero Zero Four
Computer Officers	— Nixies Zero Zero Five and
	— Nixies Zero Zero Two
Armaments Officer	— Nixies Zero Zero Three
Cargo and Tractor Beam Officer	— Nixies Zero Zero Six

Other Personnel: None.

VEHICLE USE

Vehicle type: Long Range Interceptor Craft.

Distance covered: 172.5 million miles.

Peak velocity used: Classified I.C. Code 11/11.
Level 4 "hyperspace projection."

Was remote control used: Yes.

If affirmative, how far from destination was remote activated:
About five million miles.

Was landing escort provided from destination: Yes.

If affirmative, how many vehicles in escort (state type): Seven:
Five Long Range Interceptor Craft;
One large Spacecraft carrier;
One small craft capable of underliquid operation.

Did vehicle land: Yes.

If affirmative, give reason for landing:
To affix one module, acting as a booster station, into surface of Planet;
To submerge one main collector module beneath 100 fathoms of liquid.

Position of landing (give coordinates): Strictly classified — I.C. Code 11/11.

Landing procedure (state briefly): The Interceptor Craft was guided into the landing by Venus Control which locked into the craft computer banks at a distance of 250,000 miles from destination.

Was armament used: Yes.

If affirmative, was this for defense: No.

If not defensive, state purpose: To drill one pylon hole to affix linked booster station into specially made foundation.

Was help given to Operations Force by Surface Intelligences: Yes.

If affirmative, how many Intelligences were involved: Ten.

If affirmative, were they Sentient Beings or robots: Sentient Beings.

If Sentient, were They in projected state, Full Aspect or other aspect: Full Aspect.

Was protective screening used: Yes.

If affirmative, for what reason: As a protection from severe cosmic ray bombardment, varying high temperatures and atmospheric pressure.

Was a module or other device left on surface: Yes, two.

If affirmative, state whether active or passive: Two active.

If active, state energy source of module or device:
    Booster: Magnetic energy from Planet and other classified energy source;
    Underliquid module: Classified energy source — I.C. Code 11/11.

State weight of module or device: Classified — I.C. Code 11/11.

If module or device was left, state capabilities and functions:
    To collect Universal Life Forces conditioned by the Planet Venus and transmit these through the booster station to a Satellite in orbit of

Terra for further use in "Operation Sunbeam" and other Operations.

If module or device was left, is it self-charging: Yes.

If module or device was left, is it self-adjusting: Yes, within limits outlined below.

Does module or device need regular attention: Yes.

If affirmative, state periods between attention: Approximately 250 terrene days.

If affirmative, state nature of this attention: To fine tune magnetic energy receivers of surface booster, check and adjust transmitter if necessary.

If affirmative, Who will attend to module or device: Technicians from Venus.

If affirmative, was agreement made with Surface Authority for this attention: Yes.

EQUIPMENT EVALUATION

Did all vehicle equipment perform to specifications: Yes.

If negative, describe malfunction:

(a) *Mechanical:* None.

(b) *Cosmotronic:* None.

(c) *Radionic:* None.

Technicians' suggestion(s) (I.C. Coding acceptable): Not applicable.

Authority to which malfunction was reported: Not applicable.

How was this malfunction reported:

(a) *By cosmotronic means:* Not applicable.

(*b*) *By telepathic means:* Not applicable.

(*c*) *By other means:* Not applicable.

How soon after discovery of malfunction was report made:
Not applicable.

If any appreciable time-lag before reporting, give reason(s) for this:
Not applicable.

Was confirmation of receipt of malfunction report received from reporting Authority: Not applicable.

How soon after malfunction report was confirmation received:
Not applicable.

How was confirmation transmitted:

(*a*) *By cosmotronic means:* Not applicable.

(*b*) *By telepathic means:* Not applicable.

(*c*) *By other means:* Not applicable.

PERSONAL PROTECTION DEVICE EVALUATION

Conditions under which personal protection device was worn:

(*a*) *In free Space:* By Nixies Zero Zero One, Nixies Zero Zero Two, Nixies Zero Zero Three and Nixies Zero Zero Six, immediately after projection until entry into Spacecraft.

(*b*) *On Planetary body:* By all Personnel.

If Planetary body, list:

Atmospheric temperature: 500 degrees F. approximately.

Surface gravity (*use Terra as 1.0*): .86.

Was full space armour needed: Yes.

Was full space armour worn: Yes.

If negative, state what other protective garment worn: Type:
Not applicable.

Under conditions worn, how was overall performance of suit:
Excellent for limited time period.

If very low temperatures were experienced, how long would heating elements and life support systems have performed:

Excellently: Not applicable.

Barely adequately: Not applicable.

If very high temperatures were experienced, how long would cooling elements and life support systems have performed:

Excellently: Approximately three terrene hours.

Barely adequately: Approximately four terrene hours.

How long was suit in use: Approximately 45 terrene minutes.
(*Special Note: Do not take into account possible recharging and refueling of life support systems in the above answers.*)

Was recharging and/or refueling of life support systems feasible under Operation conditions: Yes.

How well did suit protect from cosmic ray bombardment:
Excellently.

Was suit equipped with an anti-gravity device: Yes.

If affirmative, how was its performance: Excellent.

How well did the suit's internal negative-ion discharge generator work: Excellently.

PERSONNEL EVALUATION

Was projection from terrestrial counterparts necessary for this flight: Yes.

If affirmative, Who projected (I.C. Code Names only):
   Nixies Zero Zero One;
   Nixies Zero Zero Two;
   Nixies Zero Zero Three;
   Nixies Zero Zero Six.

PROJECTION DATA ON: Nixies Zero Zero One.

(a) *Time preparation commenced:*   14:00 hours P.S.T., March 8, 1980 — Earth Year 16.245.

(b) *Time of division (projection):*   14:15 hours P.S.T.

(c) *If projecting from fourth aspect, list difficulties encountered to make up to Full Aspect:*
   Detachment from surroundings;
   Rise of Kundalini, especially if Adept in depleted physical condition;
   Charging and de-charging of lower Psychic Centres.

(d) *Time of return to fourth aspect:*   15:55 hours P.S.T.

(e) *List difficulties encountered in returning to fourth aspect:*
   Detachment from Full Aspect of a part of the consciousness and re-attachment of this part of the consciousness to a base physical structure which has been inactive for a certain time, causes extreme coldness and severe neuro-physical strain.

PROJECTION DATA ON: Nixies Zero Zero Two.

(a) *Time preparation commenced:*   13:50 hours P.S.T., March 8, 1980 — Earth Year 16.245.

(b) *Time of division (projection):*   14:15 hours P.S.T.

(c) *If projecting from fourth aspect, list difficulties encountered to make up to Full Aspect:*
   Detachment from surroundings;
   Rise of Kundalini, especially if Adept in depleted physical condition;
   Charging and de-charging of lower Psychic Centres.

(d) *Time of return to fourth aspect:* 15:55 hours P.S.T.

(e) *List difficulties encountered in returning to fourth aspect:*
Detachment from Full Aspect of a part of the consciousness and re-attachment of this part of the consciousness to a base physical structure which has been inactive for a certain time, causes extreme coldness and severe neuro-physical strain.

PROJECTION DATA ON: Nixies Zero Zero Three.

(a) *Time preparation commenced:* 13:45 hours P.S.T., March 8, 1980 — Earth Year 16.245.

(b) *Time of division (projection):* 14:15 hours P.S.T.

(c) *If projecting from fourth aspect, list difficulties encountered to make up to Full Aspect:*
Detachment from surroundings;
Rise of Kundalini, especially if Adept in depleted physical condition;
Charging and de-charging of lower Psychic Centres.

(d) *Time of return to fourth aspect:* 15:55 hours P.S.T.

(e) *List difficulties encountered in returning to fourth aspect:*
Detachment from Full Aspect of a part of the consciousness and re-attachment of this part of the consciousness to a base physical structure which has been inactive for a certain time, causes extreme coldness and severe neuro-physical strain.

PROJECTION DATA ON: Nixies Zero Zero Six.

(a) *Time preparation commenced:* 14:00 hours P.S.T., March 8, 1980 — Earth Year 16.245.

(b) *Time of division (projection):* 14:15 hours P.S.T.

(c) *If projecting from fourth aspect, list difficulties encountered to make up to Full Aspect:*
Detachment from surroundings;
Rise of Kundalini, especially if Adept in depleted physical condition;

Charging and de-charging of lower Psychic Centres.

(d) *Time of return to fourth aspect:* 15:55 hours P.S.T.

(e) *List difficulties encountered in returning to fourth aspect:*
Detachment from Full Aspect of a part of the consciousness and re-attachment of this part of the consciousness to a base physical structure which has been inactive for a certain time, causes extreme coldness and severe neuro-physical strain.

Where did Projected Forms pick up operational vehicle:

(a) *At a predetermined destination with a static vehicle:* No.

(b) *With vehicle in flight:* Yes.

(c) *If (b) affirmative, how far was projection from physical body to vehicle:* Between 100,000 and 200,000 miles.

(d) *If (b) affirmative, state reason(s) why this was done:*
In order to protect the terrene Level One physical structure by reducing the time out of the terrene Level One physical body.

Were there any injuries to Sentient Beings on this flight: No.

If affirmative, when was injury(s) noticed: Not applicable.

If affirmative, give full particulars of injury(s), no matter how minor:
Not applicable.

If affirmative, state reason(s) as to cause of injury(s):
Not applicable.

What measures were taken to rectify this:

(a) *At time noticed:* Not applicable.

(b) *In future Operations:* Not applicable.

When was injury(s) treated: Not applicable.

Where was injury(s) treated: Not applicable.

Was this injury(s) reported to a Higher Authority: Not applicable.

How was this injury(s) reported:

(a) *By cosmotronic means:* Not applicable.

(b) *By telepathic means:* Not applicable.

(c) *By other means:* Not applicable.

How soon after discovery of injury(s) was report made:
Not applicable.

If any appreciable time-lag before reporting, give reason(s) for this:
Not applicable.

Was confirmation of receipt of injury(s) report received from reporting Authority: Not applicable.

How soon after injury(s) report was confirmation received:
Not applicable.

How was confirmation transmitted:

(a) *By cosmotronic means:* Not applicable.

(b) *By telepathic means:* Not applicable.

(c) *By other means:* Not applicable.

OPERATIONAL PHASE LOG
- PHASE FOUR -

Operation Name: SPACE MAGIC.

Phase number: Four.

Date: March 9, 1980; Earth Year 16.246.

Nature of Operation: Placement of remote module tuned to Satellite in orbit of Terra.

Operational destination: Neptune.

Authorizing Authority(s):   The Supreme Council on Saturn; The Interplanetary Confederation; The Protectors Of The Ineffable Flame Of The Logos Of Terra.

Date of authorization: Early 1975; Earth Year 11.

Authorization applied for by — (I.C. Code Names only):
Nixies Zero Zero One;
Nixies Zero Zero Two;
Nixies Zero Zero Three;
Nixies Zero Zero Four;
Nixies Zero Zero Five;
Nixies Zero Zero Six.
(All in Full Aspect.)

Estimated time for this Operation to be in effect:
1,000+ terrene years.

Position and Authority of annalist:
Primary Terrestrial Mental Channel, reference I.C. Authorization.

OPERATIONAL DATA

Operational Personnel by rank and name (I.C. Code Names only):

Captain	— Nixies Zero Zero One
Chief Navcom Officer	— Nixies Zero Zero Two
Second Navcom Officer	— Nixies Zero Zero Four
Computer Officers	— Nixies Zero Zero Five and
	— Nixies Zero Zero Two
Armaments Officer	— Nixies Zero Zero Three
Cargo and Tractor Beam Officer	— Nixies Zero Zero Six

Other Personnel: None.

VEHICLE USE

Vehicle type: Long Range Interceptor Craft.

Distance covered: 5,640.5 million miles.

Peak velocity used: Classified I.C. Code 11/11.
Level 4 "hyperspace projection."

Was remote control used: Yes.

If affirmative, how far from destination was remote activated:
10 million miles.

Was landing escort provided from destination: Yes.

If affirmative, how many vehicles in escort (state type): Seven:
Six Long Range Interceptor Craft;
One Spacecraft Carrier.

Did vehicle land: Yes.

If affirmative, give reason for landing: To affix module into surface of Planet.

Position of landing (give coordinates): Strictly classified — I.C. Code 11/11.

Landing procedure (state briefly): The Interceptor Craft was guided into the landing by Neptune Control on Triton which locked into the craft computer banks at a distance of 10 million miles from destination.

Was armament used: Yes.

If affirmative, was this for defense: No.

If not defensive, state purpose: To drill four pylon holes to affix module structure into foundation.

Was help given to Operations Force by Surface Intelligences:
Yes, help offered.

If affirmative, how many Intelligences were involved: Twelve.

If affirmative, were they Sentient Beings or robots:
Nine Sentient Beings;
Three robots.

If Sentient, were They in projected state, Full Aspect or other aspect: Full Aspect.

Was protective screening used: Yes.

If affirmative, for what reason: As a protection from cosmic ray bombardment, magnetic disturbances and low temperatures.

Was a module or other device left on surface: Yes, one.

If affirmative, state whether active or passive: Active.

If active, state energy source of module or device:
Solar energy batteries, recharged from tracking solar panels;
Magnetic energy from the Planet.

State weight of module or device: Classified — I.C. Code 11/11.

If module or device was left, state capabilities and functions:
To collect Universal Life Forces conditioned by the Planet Neptune and transmit these to a Satellite in orbit of Terra for further use in "Operation Sunbeam" and other Operations.

If module or device was left, is it self-charging: Yes.

If module or device was left, is it self-adjusting: Yes, within limits outlined below.

Does module or device need regular attention: Yes.

If affirmative, state periods between attention: Approximately 364 terrene days.

If affirmative, state nature of this attention: To fine tune solar energy receivers, fine tune magnetic energy receivers, check and adjust transmitter if necessary.

If affirmative, Who will attend to module or device: Technicians from either Jupiter or Saturn.

If affirmative, was agreement made with Surface Authority for this attention: Yes.

EQUIPMENT EVALUATION

Did all vehicle equipment perform to specifications: No.

If negative, describe malfunction:

(a) *Mechanical:* No.

(b) *Cosmotronic:* Yes.

(c) *Radionic:* Yes.

Technicians' suggestion(s) (I.C. Coding acceptable):
Replace natural and cultured sapphires on gravity detection board, as these crystals broke down under normal acceleration. Suggest replacing with I.C. Code reference L-9 or equivalent. (Note 1.)

Authority to which malfunction was reported: The Supreme Council on Saturn.

How was this malfunction reported:

(a) *By cosmotronic means:* Yes.

(b) *By telepathic means:* Yes.

(c) *By other means:* No.

How soon after discovery of malfunction was report made:
Immediately.

If any appreciable time-lag before reporting, give reason(s) for this:
Not applicable.

Was confirmation of receipt of malfunction report received from reporting Authority: Yes.

How soon after malfunction report was confirmation received:
Within minutes.

How was confirmation transmitted:

(a) *By cosmotronic means:* Yes.

(b) *By telepathic means:* Yes.

(c) *By other means:* No.

PERSONAL PROTECTION DEVICE EVALUATION

Conditions under which personal protection device was worn:

(a) *In free Space:* By Nixies Zero Zero One, Nixies Zero Zero Two, Nixies Zero Zero Three and Nixies Zero Zero Six, immediately after projection until entry into Spacecraft.

(b) *On Planetary body:* By all Personnel.

If Planetary body, list:

  Atmospheric temperature: Minus 330 degrees F.

  Surface gravity (use Terra as 1.0): 1.12.

Was full space armour needed: Yes.

Was full space armour worn: Yes.

If negative, state what other protective garment worn: Type:
Not applicable.

Under conditions worn, how was overall performance of suit:
Excellent.

If very low temperatures were experienced, how long would heating elements and life support systems have performed:

Excellently: Approximately 10 terrene hours.

Barely adequately: Approximately 12 terrene hours.

If very high temperatures were experienced, how long would cooling elements and life support systems have performed:

Excellently: Not applicable.

Barely adequately: Not applicable.

How long was suit in use: Approximately 20-30 terrene minutes.
(*Special Note:* Do not take into account possible recharging and refueling of life support systems in the above answers.)

Was recharging and/or refueling of life support systems feasible under Operation conditions: Yes.

How well did suit protect from cosmic ray bombardment:
Excellently.

Was suit equipped with an anti-gravity device: Yes.

If affirmative, how was its performance: Excellent.

How well did the suit's internal negative-ion discharge generator work: Excellently.

PERSONNEL EVALUATION

Was projection from terrestrial counterparts necessary for this flight: Yes.

If affirmative, Who projected (I.C. Code Names only):
   Nixies Zero Zero One;
   Nixies Zero Zero Two;
   Nixies Zero Zero Three;
   Nixies Zero Zero Six.

PROJECTION DATA ON: Nixies Zero Zero One.

(a) *Time preparation commenced:*   14:15 hours P.S.T., March 9, 1980 — Earth Year 16.246.

(b) *Time of division (projection):*   14:30 hours P.S.T.

(c) *If projecting from fourth aspect, list difficulties encountered to make up to Full Aspect:*
   Detachment from surroundings;
   Rise of Kundalini, especially if Adept in depleted physical condition;
   Charging and de-charging of lower Psychic Centres.

(d) *Time of return to fourth aspect:*   15:41 hours P.S.T.

(e) *List difficulties encountered in returning to fourth aspect:*
   Detachment from Full Aspect of a part of the consciousness and re-attachment of this part of the consciousness to a base physical structure which has been inactive for a certain time, causes extreme coldness and severe neuro-physical strain.

PROJECTION DATA ON: Nixies Zero Zero Two.

(a) *Time preparation commenced:*   14:05 hours P.S.T., March 9, 1980 — Earth Year 16.246.

(b) *Time of division (projection):*   14:30 hours P.S.T.

(c) *If projecting from fourth aspect, list difficulties encountered to make up to Full Aspect:*
   Detachment from surroundings;
   Rise of Kundalini, especially if Adept in depleted physical condition;
   Charging and de-charging of lower Psychic Centres.

(d) *Time of return to fourth aspect:* 15:41 hours P.S.T.

(e) *List difficulties encountered in returning to fourth aspect:*
   Detachment from Full Aspect of a part of the consciousness and re-attachment of this part of the consciousness to a base physical structure which has been inactive for a certain time, causes extreme coldness and severe neuro-physical strain.

PROJECTION DATA ON: Nixies Zero Zero Three.

(a) *Time preparation commenced:* 14:00 hours P.S.T., March 9, 1980 — Earth Year 16.246.

(b) *Time of division (projection):* 14:30 hours P.S.T.

(c) *If projecting from fourth aspect, list difficulties encountered to make up to Full Aspect:*
   Detachment from surroundings;
   Rise of Kundalini, especially if Adept in depleted physical condition;
   Charging and de-charging of lower Psychic Centres.

(d) *Time of return to fourth aspect:* 15:41 hours P.S.T.

(e) *List difficulties encountered in returning to fourth aspect:*
   Detachment from Full Aspect of a part of the consciousness and re-attachment of this part of the consciousness to a base physical structure which has been inactive for a certain time, causes extreme coldness and severe neuro-physical strain.

PROJECTION DATA ON: Nixies Zero Zero Six.

(a) *Time preparation commenced:* 14:15 hours P.S.T., March 9, 1980 — Earth Year 16.246.

(b) *Time of division (projection):* 14:30 hours P.S.T.

(c) *If projecting from fourth aspect, list difficulties encountered to make up to Full Aspect:*
   Detachment from surroundings;
   Rise of Kundalini, especially if Adept in depleted physical condition;
   Charging and de-charging of lower Psychic Centres.

(d) *Time of return to fourth aspect:* 15:41 hours P.S.T.

(e) *List difficulties encountered in returning to fourth aspect:*
   Detachment from Full Aspect of a part of the consciousness and re-attachment of this part of the consciousness to a base physical structure which has been inactive for a certain time, causes extreme coldness and severe neuro-physical strain.

Where did Projected Forms pick up operational vehicle:

(a) *At a predetermined destination with a static vehicle:* No.

(b) *With vehicle in flight:* Yes.

(c) *If (b) affirmative, how far was projection from physical body to vehicle:* Between 100,000 and 200,000 miles.

(d) *If (b) affirmative, state reason(s) why this was done:*
   In order to protect the terrene Level One physical structure by reducing the time out of the terrene Level One physical body.

Were there any injuries to Sentient Beings on this flight: No.

If affirmative, when was injury(s) noticed: Not applicable.

If affirmative, give full particulars of injury(s), no matter how minor:
   Not applicable.

If affirmative, state reason(s) as to cause of injury(s):
   Not applicable.

What measures were taken to rectify this:

(a) *At time noticed:* Not applicable.

(*b*) *In future Operations:*   Not applicable.

When was injury(s) treated: Not applicable.

Where was injury(s) treated: Not applicable.

Was this injury(s) reported to Higher Authority: Not applicable.

How was this injury(s) reported:

(*a*)   *By cosmotronic means:*   Not applicable.

(*b*)   *By telepathic means:*   Not applicable.

(*c*)   *By other means:*   Not applicable.

How soon after discovery of injury(s) was report made:

Not applicable.

If any appreciable time-lag before reporting, give reason(s) for this:
Not applicable.

Was confirmation of receipt of injury(s) report received from reporting Authority: Not applicable.

How soon after injury(s) report was confirmation received:
Not applicable.

How was confirmation transmitted:

(*a*)   *By cosmotronic means:*   Not applicable.

(*b*)   *By telepathic means:*   Not applicable.

(*c*)   *By other means:*   Not applicable.

****

NOTE 1. The circuit board in question is interfaced with the main Navcom computer system. As both cultured and natural sapphires are affected by gravitational forces, the effect, however minor, can be measured cosmotronically and produces an exact acceleration reference. Both the cultured and natural sapphires broke down. The cosmotronic circuit incorporated into the system to revive the cultured sapphires could not function correctly as the final irreversible breakdown was too rapid.

OPERATIONAL PHASE LOG
- PHASE FIVE -

Operation Name: SPACE MAGIC.

Phase number: Five.

Date: January 23rd, 1981; Earth Year 17.200.

Nature of Operation: Placement of Satellite into stable orbit of Terra.

Estimated duration of orbit: 1,000 + terrene years.

Operational destination: Terrene orbit.

Authorizing Authority(s): The Supreme Council on Saturn;
The Interplanetary Confederation;
The Protectors Of The Ineffable Flame Of The Logos Of Terra.

Protecting Authority: The Supreme Council on Saturn, through Satellite No. 3.

Date of authorization: Early 1975; Earth Year 11.

Authorization applied for by — (I.C. Code Names only):
   Nixies Zero Zero One;   — Nixies Zero Zero Four;
   Nixies Zero Zero Two;   — Nixies Zero Zero Five;
   Nixies Zero Zero Three; — Nixies Zero Zero Six.
            (All in Full Aspect.)

Estimated time for this Operation to be in effect:
   1,000 + terrene years.

Position and Authority of annalist:
   Primary Terrestrial Mental Channel, reference I.C. Authorization.

OPERATIONAL DATA

Operational Personnel by rank and name (I.C. Code Names only):

Captain	— Nixies Zero Zero One
Chief Navcom Officer	— Nixies Zero Zero Two
Second Navcom Officer	— Nixies Zero Zero Four
Computer Officers	— Nixies Zero Zero Five and
	— Nixies Zero Zero Two
Armaments Officer	— Nixies Zero Zero Three
Cargo and Tractor Beam Officer	— Nixies Zero Zero Six

Other Personnel: None.

VEHICLE USE

Vehicle type: Long Range Interceptor Craft.

Distance covered: Classified — I.C. Code 11/11.

Peak velocity used: Classified information — I.C. Code 11/11.

Was remote control used: No.

If affirmative, how far from destination was remote activated:
Not applicable.

Was landing escort provided from destination: Not applicable.

If affirmative, how many vehicles in escort (state type):
Not applicable.

Did vehicle land: No.

If affirmative, give reason for landing: Not applicable.

Position of landing (give coordinates): Not applicable.

Landing procedure (state briefly): Not applicable.

Was armament used: No, magnetic tractor beam only.

If affirmative, was this for defense: Not applicable.

If not defensive, state purpose: For transportation of Satellite.

Was help given to Operations Force by Surface Intelligences: No.

If affirmative, how many Intelligences were involved: Not applicable.

If affirmative, were they Sentient Beings or robots: Neither were used.

If Sentient, were They in projected state, Full Aspect or other aspect: Not applicable.

Was protective screening used: Yes.

If affirmative, for what reason:
1. For normal travelling safety of main transport vehicle;
2. Around Satellite, internally generated photon screening to render the Satellite visibly undetectable by terrestrial radar and radio telescopes.

Was a module or other device left: Yes, orbiting Satellite.

If affirmative, state whether active or passive: Active.

If active, state energy source of Satellite:
Solar energy batteries recharged from tracking solar panels; Magnetic energy from Terra.

State weight of Satellite: Classified — I.C. Code 11/11.

If Satellite was left, state capabilities and functions:
Capable of picking up Energies from the Psychic Centres of the Planets Saturn, Jupiter, Venus and Neptune, which are radiated by the fixed modules, and then transmitting these, on demand, when activated by pre-set classified coded instructions. This code instructs the micro-computers on board the Satellite as to which set of instruments are activated. Depending upon which specific code is used, the receivers on board are relieved of their normal isolation and are then

placed in tune with any or all of the modules previously placed upon Saturn, Jupiter, Venus or Neptune. Dependent on the code used, the on-board computers will transmit an activation signal to the relevant Planetary module. This energy can then be collected by the Masters from Gotha or other Agencies Who have gained the required permission, and stored in Their on-board batteries. The correct classified code is the only impulse which can activate the system. The Satellite can be ordered to self-destruct or move out of Planetary orbit by use of the correct coding system.

Does Satellite have any evasive abilities: Yes.

If affirmative, give brief description of these abilities:
The Satellite is equipped with detector apparatus which is capable of detecting any missile sent against it, or any foreign body in its orbital path. This detector apparatus is capable of relaying information to the controlling on-board computers, which in turn can activate a propulsion unit which will make alterations in its pre-set course so that the Satellite will avoid collision. The memory banks in these computers will then direct the Satellite back into its predetermined orbit.

If a specialized course computer is incorporated in the Satellite, is this also capable of correcting for magnetic disturbances: Yes.

If affirmative, give brief, non-classified description of the capabilities of this computer: The computer is capable of correcting for any orbital deviations which may be caused by gravitational or magnetic disturbances within the Solar System.

If Satellite was left, is it self-charging: Yes.

If Satellite was left, is it self-adjusting: Yes, within limits.

Does Satellite need regular attention: Yes, it may. (Not under normal conditions.)

If affirmative, state periods between attention: Not known yet.
Careful periodic examination will be conducted to ascertain service periods, if any.

If affirmative, state nature of this attention: Although all systems are capable of being charged by natural magnetic influences and solar radiation, if one or all of these systems did fail, these can be remotely reactivated.

If affirmative, Who will attend to Satellite: Technicians from Satellite No. 3.

If affirmative, was agreement made with Authority for this attention: Yes.

EQUIPMENT EVALUATION

Did all vehicle equipment perform to specifications: Yes.

If negative, describe malfunction:

(*a*) *Mechanical:* Not applicable.

(*b*) *Cosmotronic:* Not applicable.

(*c*) *Radionic:* Not applicable.

Technicians' suggestion(s) (I.C. Coding acceptable): Not applicable.

Authority to which malfunction was reported: Not applicable.

How was this malfunction reported:

(*a*) *By cosmotronic means:* Not applicable.

(*b*) *By telepathic means:* Not applicable.

(*c*) *By other means:* Not applicable.

How soon after discovery of malfunction was report made:
Not applicable.

If any appreciable time-lag before reporting, give reason(s) for this:
Not applicable.

Was confirmation of receipt of malfunction report received from reporting Authority: Not applicable.

How soon after malfunction report was confirmation received: Not applicable.

How was confirmation transmitted:

(a) *By cosmotronic means:* Not applicable.

(b) *By telepathic means:* Not applicable.

(c) *By other means:* Not applicable.

PERSONAL PROTECTION DEVICE EVALUATION

Conditions under which personal protection device was worn: Device not worn.

(a) *In free Space:* Not applicable.

(b) *On Planetary body:* Not applicable.

If Planetary body, list:

    Atmospheric temperature: Not applicable.

    Surface gravity (*use Terra as 1.0*): Not applicable.

Was full space armour needed: Not applicable.

Was full space armour worn: Not applicable.

If negative, state what other protective garment worn: Type: Not applicable.

Under conditions worn, how was overall performance of suit: Not applicable.

If very low temperatures were experienced, how long would heating elements and life support systems have performed:

    Excellently: Not applicable.

"Operation Sunbeam" — Phase 116: August 23rd/24th, 1981, 11:01 p.m. — 1:01 a.m.; Spiritual Energies relayed from module on Jupiter via Satellite.

FURTHER SATELLITE USAGE

Either three or four times each year, a Spacecraft comes into orbit of the Planet Earth in order to transmit Spiritual Energies to all Levels of sentient life on or connected to this Earth. During these times, all unselfish Spiritual actions for the benefit of others are enhanced 3,000 times because of the individual attention paid to those who, with a completely pure motive, are working in a Spiritual way for the benefit and upliftment of their fellow men.

These dates are given before the operation of this Spacecraft and are published in The Aetherius Society Journal called *Cosmic Voice*, and are available to all people, irrespective of whether they are Members or not, who care to subscribe. (Note 2.)

This Spacecraft is large by Earth standards, being over a mile and a half from bow to stern, and is filled with sophisticated instrumentation. The Operators of this Spacecraft, given the code name of "Satellite No. 3", are capable of sending Spiritual Energies down to an individual, a group of individuals, or even a country, in the exact degree that people are able to use these Energies with a pure motive of helping their fellow men. These Energies are transmitted in a frequency predetermined by the receivers' capabilities of using them.

The operation of this Spacecraft is termed a "Magnetization Period" or "Spiritual Push."

The Levels referred to in the following log denote the Levels of sentient existence directly connected to this Planet. Taking the physical realms, as we know them, as Level One, there are six Levels of life above this, commonly termed as the "higher realms", and several Levels below Level One, commonly termed as the "lower astral realms."

In the following log, the reader will see that the Satellite launched by The Six Adepts on January 23rd, 1981 was used by Cosmic Intelligences from Satellite No. 3 on two definite occasions.

SPECIFIC SATELLITE USAGE IN MAGNETIZATION PERIODS

Spiritual Push No. 1 for 1981:

Saturday, May 23rd, 1981, 2:00 p.m. — 3:00 p.m.

Spiritual Energy radiated through Satellite from Venus to Levels Three, Five and Six: .001% through the Spiritual Energy Radiator to Level One.

Saturday, May 23rd, 1981, 3:00 p.m. — 4:00 p.m.

Spiritual Energy radiated through Satellite from Jupiter to Levels Three, Five and Six: .001% through the Spiritual Energy Radiator to Level One. (Note 3.)

SATELLITE USAGE IN A SPECIAL MISSION FOR WORLD PEACE

In September 1981, a new Mission for stabilization of the Devic realms and for world balance and peace was launched by the Highest Authority in this Solar System, namely, The Lords Of Saturn. (Note 4.) This was performed by the author and a hand-picked crew in the North of Scotland, British Isles, operating directly over one of the most important Psychic Centres in the Body of the Planet Earth.

Little has been published to date regarding this Mission because certain important aspects of the Mission have been strictly classified. Therefore, at the time of writing, it is not possible to give much detail about this Mission, save to state that the Satellite launched by The Six Adepts on January 23rd, 1981, was used in two Sub-Phases of this vitally important new Mission.

SATELLITE USAGE IN THE MISSION FOR WORLD PEACE

Friday, September 11th, 1981, Sub-Phase 1 — not used.

Saturday, September 12th, 1981, Sub-Phase 2:

Spiritual Energies from Neptune were injected into the natural pattern around Earth via the Satellite.

Sunday, September 13th, 1981, Sub-Phase 3:

Spiritual Energies from Saturn were injected into the natural pattern around Earth via the Satellite. (Note 5.)

OPERATION SPACE MAGIC

In the natural course of events there always has been an interchange of subtle energies between Planetary Bodies within this Solar System. Some energies are impinged upon and penetrate the surfaces of Planetary Bodies, even from distant Galaxies. The ethers of vast Space, act as a vehicle through which subtle energies of different frequencies are continually travelling to and from worldly masses, to be absorbed, changed and transmitted by them.

Many thinkers have proved that energies, continually emitted by other Planets within this Solar System, not only affect the natural environment of this Earth, but also affect the destinies of the inhabitants. But since "Operation Space Magic", certain Spiritual Energies from Saturn, Jupiter, Venus and Neptune can be given in a controlled form which does not happen in the normal course of nature. While these energies through the Satellite will never be, in their pure state, directed to individual earthlings, the fact that they can be directed to The Logos of the Planet Herself, brings about a Karmic manipulation which will be of great benefit to all Levels of life on Earth.

"Operation Space Magic" will never interfere with the so-called "free will" of the inhabitants of Earth, but on the contrary, will help terrestrial conditions in such a way as to allow the masses to become more evolved, providing that they choose to use their inherent God-given potential in the correct manner.

In the years to come the Spiritual results of "Operation Space Magic" will be very great. We should all thank God for the help given to us by the Six Interplanetary Adepts Who designed and performed this Mission on our behalf.

AUTHOR'S RECOMMENDATIONS

NOTE 1. Further understanding of the vitally important Cosmic Mission, "Operation Sunbeam", can be gained by a study of the following Aetherius Society publications:

Cassette No.C-54, *Operation Sunbeam;* Metacassette® No.MC-2, *Operation Sunbeam Inspires The Galaxy!* —a Transmission from a Cosmic Master explaining the immense influence of this Mission; and Metacassette® No. MC-19, *Gotha Speaks To Earth*—another Transmission describing the reason for the presence on Earth of advanced Intelligences from the Solar System "Gotha" to help in "Operation Sunbeam."

The booklet, *Operation Sunbeam — God's Magic In Action,* reveals the astounding Karmic repercussions of the Mission and contains the report of a meeting, attended by the author, of The Spiritual Hierarchy Of Earth to establish Their involvement in "Operation Sunbeam."

The history of "Operation Sunbeam" has also been recorded in *The Aetherius Society Newsletter,* later replaced by the Journal, *Cosmic Voice.* Details are obtainable from the publishers, The Aetherius Society.

NOTE 2. For further information on Satellite No. 3, readers are recommended to study the book, *The Nine Freedoms,* by the same author, pages 85-92, which contain a detailed description, with diagrams, of the Spacecraft itself and its function.

Full information explaining the vital importance of co-operation with the orbital times of this Spacecraft is available in early Issues of the magazine, *Cosmic Voice,* details of which are available from The Aetherius Society.

Statistical information on the operation of Satellite No. 3 is contained in the booklet, *Operation Sunbeam — God's Magic In Action.*

NOTE 3. A Spiritual Energy Radiator is a specially designed piece of radionic apparatus, capable of receiving a beam of subtle energy and transmitting this energy in pulses. During every Magnetization Period, The Aetherius Society runs their Spiritual Energy Radiators in

America and England for a given period, generally about three hours per day each machine. Sometimes instructions are given to increase this normal running time, which happened in May 1981, and during that time, a small percentage of Spiritual Energies, picked up by Satellite No. 3 from the Satellite put up by The Six Adepts, were conveyed through the Spiritual Energy Radiator and re-transmitted.

The whole action of the Spiritual Energy Radiators is governed by strict Karmic Law, in that, if these machines were not available, mankind would have to be deprived of millions of units of Spiritual Energy because of the exact law of action and reaction which governs all facets of life.

Each of the Spiritual Energy Radiators in England and America transmits 6,120 Prayer Hours of energy during their three hours of daily operation during each Magnetization Period. In 1981, the cumulative energy through these magnificent radionic machines amounted to 1,541,560 (one million, five hundred and forty-one thousand, five hundred and sixty) Prayer Hours of the highest quality of Spiritual Energy that is capable of being used on this physical plane.

Ten men praying for eight hours a day, 350 days a year, from age 21 on, would have to spend their entire (average) lives to transmit this amount of energy.

NOTE 4. For a greater understanding of the most elevated and highly evolved Lords Of Saturn, readers are recommended to study Chapter 8 of *The Nine Freedoms,* entitled "The Eighth Freedom Will Be Saturnian Existence", available from The Aetherius Society.

NOTE 5. The only report available on the new Mission at the time of publication is contained in The Aetherius Society Journal, *Cosmic Voice,* Volume 3, Issues 1 & 2, January 1982.

This Mission will be continued by Saturn Supreme Command from time to time in different parts of the world in order to bring about a Devic stabilization which will directly help other forms of life on this Planet, in that the Devic realms are dependent on the energy output of sentient life forms, hence the violent and quickly changeable weather conditions experienced by man.

To further understand this complex science, study cassette No. C-57, *The Devic Kingdom,* and "The Fifth Blessing" from the book, *The Twelve Blessings,* is recommended. These are available from the publishers, The Aetherius Society.